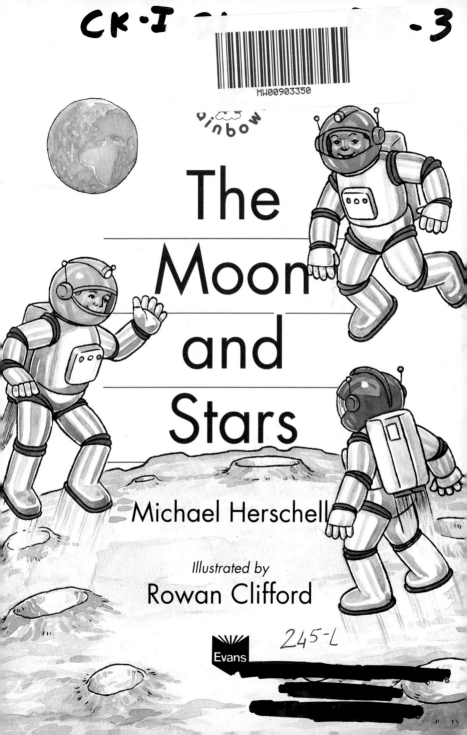

The Moon and Stars

Michael Herschell

Illustrated by
Rowan Clifford

Evans

The Moon is our nearest neighbour in space. But it is still 385,000 kilometres away.

I wish we could visit the Moon and stars.

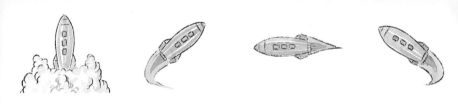

You *can* visit the Moon and stars. Climb into the magic spaceship and let's go!

6

8

Earth is one of nine planets
that go around the Sun.

Together the planets and
the Sun are called the
Solar System.

10

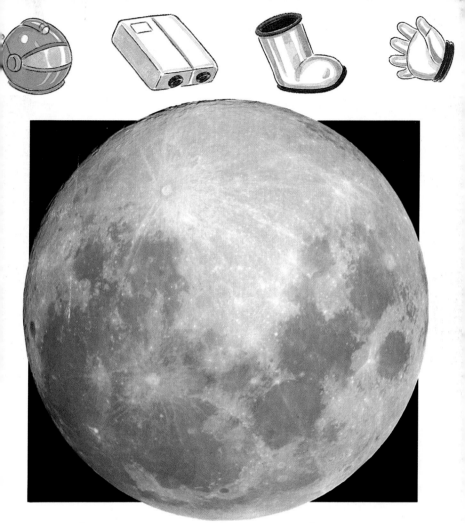

Nothing can live on the
Moon because there is no
air or water.

12

Your body is much lighter on the Moon. That is why you can jump so easily.

That is
Mars.
Mars is a dry, rocky planet.
It is also very, very cold.

Jupiter

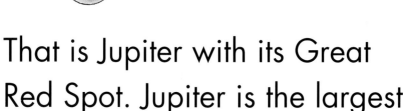

That is Jupiter with its Great
Red Spot. Jupiter is the largest
planet in the Solar System.

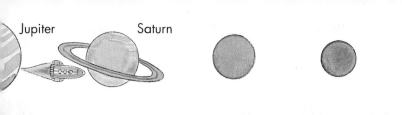

Jupiter Saturn

The rings of Saturn are made
of pieces of ice and dust.

19

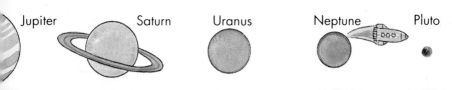

Jupiter Saturn Uranus Neptune Pluto

And there is little Pluto.

Pluto is about the size of our Moon. It takes 248 years for Pluto to go around the Sun.

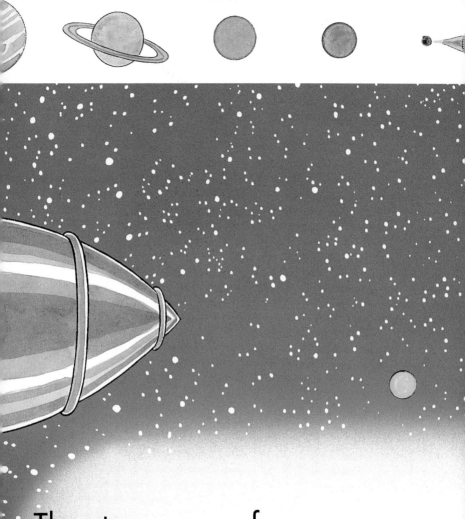

The stars are so far away.
We must travel very fast to get
to the nearest one. Hold tight!

Groups of stars are called galaxies. There are thousands and thousands of galaxies. Our galaxy is called the Milky Way.

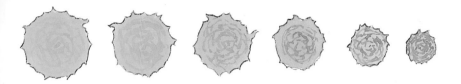

No, stars are all different sizes. The large stars are called supergiants. The small stars are called dwarfs.

Our Sun is quite a small star.

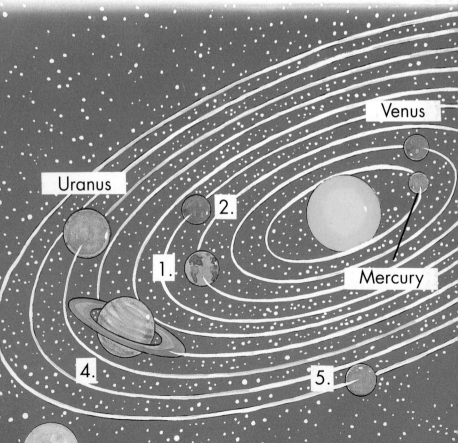

Four of the planets have been
named. Can you name the
other five?

Venus

Uranus

2.

1.

Mercury

4.

5.

1. Earth 2. Mars 3. Jupiter 4. Saturn 5. Pluto